Ad Tech & Programmatic

Master the technologies involved in the online media
channel and excel in programmatic advertising

Julian Delphiki

Ad Tech and Programmatic / Julian Delphiki – 1st Edition

ISBN 979-8643286912

Index

Part I

Ad Tech

1. Introduction

Digital advertising refers to all paid promotional messaging that's displayed on desktop computers, laptops, tablets, mobile phones and other Internet-connected devices. For many content-based websites, hosting ads is the primary source of revenue.

New and developing technologies in particular are driving the continued growth of digital advertising, with the ever-increasing use of mobile devices, video streaming and audio formats such as music and podcasts.

Advertising technology – or 'ad tech' - today enables increasingly personalized campaigns, as an individual viewer's response to specific messaging can be recorded, analyzed and optimized for future enhancements.

But how does it all work... and who's involved? How are campaigns planned? And what does 'success' look like in digital advertising?

1.1. Digital advertising

The marketplace for digital advertising is huge, with spending levels now surpassing television advertising. In fact, global digital ad spending now easily exceeds $300 billion per year, with one third going to mobile, and over one third being spent in the United States.

Google, including YouTube; Facebook, including Instagram; and Alibaba are the biggest sellers of digital ads, together accounting for just over 62% of the global market.

Today, the majority of digital advertising is traded 'programmatically', which is to say that ads are traded in real-time via an automated auction process, and powered by huge amounts of data.

We'll be examining the specific technologies that power this system in more detail, but for now we'll be viewing things from the general perspective of how and why a specific ad appears to a user in a certain place and at a certain time - something known as an 'ad impression'.

If you're 'involved' in digital advertising, you're likely to be either an advertiser, a publisher, a user, or a data provider…

For an Advertiser, a primary concern is: "I have this ad, it's pretty good and I want to put it somewhere it'll be seen by my target audience". They're looking? to buy ad space: they are the "demand side". Now, Publishers have what advertisers are looking for. They run sites, and a thought on their mind is: "I have all these sites, and on these sites, I have all this space that I could put ads in". They're looking to sell ad space. They are the "supply side".

So, advertisers and publishers are the perfect match, right? Well, generally, yes, but not necessarily. Let's face it, it's highly unlikely that an ad for a new leather jacket and a vegan living online magazine are going to work well together and receive a positive response from the user.

Users, of course, are those that visit websites or use apps. They are the 'audience'… and the target for digital advertising, and if you were to ask them about what they want and expect from the ads they're served, they'd likely all say the same kind of thing: "They should be relevant to me".

This is where data providers come in. Data providers are third party vendors that can help both advertisers and publishers to strike the best deal. Whether it concerns the content of a publisher's site, or the behavior and demographics of users, data providers collect and sell information – information that can be used to figure out which combinations of ads and ad spaces will best cater to the needs and interests of users.

The actual buying of ad space can be done in-house, or outsourced to an agency - a company with expertise in planning, creating, buying and managing advertising on behalf of its clients.

When deals are arranged directly between an individual advertiser and publisher - these ad placements are referred to as "guaranteed". They're guaranteed because publishers sign on a dotted line and make a commitment to deliver a specified number of ad impressions for a specified price.

Advertisers and publishers can also do business through ad networks. Ad networks can be seen as a kind of middleman, connecting advertisers with a range of publishers who have available inventory that meets the advertisers' needs.

Ad networks often handle 'remnant' inventory, which is space left over after more 'premium' inventory has been sold, and they often do so programmatically – in the respect that automation is involved in the way that the inventory is dealt.

Ad exchanges provide another means of buying and selling ad inventory. These are programmatic marketplaces, used by all players in the digital advertising space - including ad networks - which allow inventory to be auctioned off, in real time, to the highest bidder.

So, we know how ad space can be bought, but how do advertisers pay for it? Actually, perhaps a better way to phrase the question is: What are advertisers really paying for?

Perhaps they're paying for clicks. The Cost per Click method of payment requires an advertiser to pay up when a user clicks on a link within their ad. It's typical within search marketing especially, and some of the more sought-after keywords can be very pricey – costing advertisers over $50 per click.

Cost per Action is similar to Cost per Click, but it goes a step further in the respect that the advertiser pays when a user clicks on their ad and completes a transaction. This is the least common payment method, and the one that poses the greatest risk

to publishers, because whether they receive payment relies entirely on the advertiser's ability to convert the user.

And lastly, predominant within display advertising, Cost per Impression calls for advertisers to pay for the number of times that their ad is displayed.

When advertisers pay by the impression, it's generally referred to as Cost per Mille or CPM as they're usually charged in units of a thousand.

1.2.   Campaigns and media planning

Now we've taken a look at how ad space is traded, it's time to explore where ads can be found...

Also known as Pay per Click, or PPC, paid search ads appear in the results pages of search engines like Google, and shopping sites such as Amazon. They're also returned to users in response to voice searches. Paid search ads are valued by advertisers because they're served to a user only after they've made a relevant query.

This almost guarantees that these users are actively interested in products or services related to the ad. In 2019, search ads have become the largest digital advertising market segment.

Display ads are banner ads, or rich media ads that utilize video and animation. They appear on websites or social media platforms, accompanying content that caters to an audience's needs or interests. Here, users are simply browsing... they're not seeking out the products or services being offered, and so, they're much less likely to click on the ad.

Mobile advertising is growing sharply, reaching 63% of total ad spend in the US back in early 2018. As access to 5G networks increases, advertisers will be able to deliver even larger high-quality videos, opening up major new opportunities.

This is especially true in China, which is not only home to a huge eCommerce marketplace, but is also a world leader in 5G connections.

Social media platforms have increasingly become channels for delivering advertising rather than free content, especially via their messaging apps.

With the number of monthly users on these apps recently overtaking the platforms themselves, social advertising is expected to grow significantly, especially with the ability to shop directly and seamlessly from their feed.

As well as being a natural medium for storytelling, video advertising has been shown to increase click-through rates, purchase intent and brand awareness.

To really maximize ad performance, an effective digital advertising strategy will typically benefit from using two or more channels. This is known as cross-channel advertising.

Different platforms offer different features and audiences, and advertisers can apply what they learn from one channel to another. For example, you could study successful PPC keywords and use them to target social media audiences interested in related topics.

With such a wide array of possible channels to choose from, it can be daunting when trying to decide which ones to implement within a digital advertising strategy.

For this reason, companies will often seek help from a media planner. They assess how impactful different types of media will be within the market their client wants to reach. Media planners will suggest important steps to take before deciding which combination of channels will be the most effective...

They might be someone working in your own company, or working for an agency on your behalf, but either way - you'll likely employ the services of a media planner.

However, it's vital that prior to this you define your goals for your campaign, making sure they are clear, measurable and realistic. Along with Key Performance Indicators, these will help you to make sure you're on track and achieving your goals. This will also assist the media planner in devising the best strategy for your company. If, for example, you wanted to increase brand awareness, it would be wise to focus on the number of times your ad impressions are seen, or your video completion rate.

Once you have a clear idea of what you are aiming for, you should look towards understanding your audience. As today's customers not only buy online, but research, review and critique products and services, it's important that advertising is as relevant and personalized to the customer as possible.

Your media planner will look to identify who your target audiences are, and then may create personas of customers to better understand their needs and motivations. This will help the planner to decide which marketing channels are likely to engage them.

It's also vital that you understand the marketplace of what you're looking to advertise. To do so, a media planner will take a look at current industry trends and gather intelligence on your competitors. They often won't obtain their exact strategies but will note the types of ads they run and the channels they use.

A consistent use of certain channels might suggest these are particularly reliable. But that's not to say lesser-used channels couldn't be successful for you... They may perhaps have never been considered and could be an untapped resource.

Having gained a clear understanding of your desired outcomes, your audiences, and the marketplace, you should be well set to begin deciding which channels and ad formats will work for your campaign.

Needless to say, the finer details of your media plan will depend on your situation and what you want to achieve, but, regardless, there are a number of considerations you'll need to work through...

When it comes to creating your media plan, first, you'll need to consider where your ad will be placed and how it will be formatted. With the help of your media planner, think about the sites your target audience are likely to visit, and where on the page your ad could be placed.

Also, consider the unique characteristics of different channels. What ad formats do different channels support? What, in particular, makes a channel especially interesting or applicable to your audience? It could be the type of influencers that frequent them, or perhaps it's popularity with a particular demographic. Make sure to keep an eye on trends and current developments, as usage of channels can always change.

Now that you've done your research and chosen your channels, the final step of media planning is to allocate your advertising budget. Think about the cost of your ads and the methods of payment. Will you be charged Cost per Click, Cost per Action or Cost per Impression? Your budget must take into account spending across the lifetime of the campaign, so consider formats and channels that you may want to use in the future... as well as ad space bought in real-time.

Once the media plan is complete, the insights gained in the planning stage can be taken by the advertiser... who can then proceed to use them.

Whilst buying ad space is now often automated, it's still crucial to have human involvement in this process. Often, this would be the work of a 'media buyer', but it's not uncommon for the media planner to also take on this role.

The media buyer must ensure that they establish relationships with individual publishers or channel owners when purchasing ad space. They're also responsible for negotiating deals to secure the required ad space within the budget.

And finally, when ads are running, they must monitor their performance and recommend changes for optimal results.

1.3.   Measuring performance

As with any strategy your business undertakes, you'll need to have a plan in place for measuring its success - weighed up against the costs and potential return on investment. Digital advertising can be very expensive, so it's important that all parties involved are able to monitor performance…

Advertisers want to be able to optimize every aspect of a campaign to achieve their goals - from increasing visitor engagement and brand awareness, to minimizing revenue loss - whilst publishers want to verify that their impressions are being sold to maximum advantage.

So how can you go about getting this information? Well, advanced analytics tools can be used to discover patterns in visitors' responses to specific ads, to derive insights and to allow for fast adjustments to campaign creative, ad placement and inventory offered.

The vast quantity of data that's available around the results of each ad placement puts particular pressure on publishers - underperforming placements could lead to a decrease in demand for their ad slots. Publishers need to clearly display their click through rates, and the number of clicks each ad generates... as well as running further analysis to really understand which ad formats, sizes and placements generate the most value. With this information, publishers are able to optimize their inventory usage in real time.

Marketers often list the main challenges of running digital advertising campaigns as obtaining actionable insights and meaningful reports - especially if those campaigns are run programmatically.

Issues that are frequently encountered include: inconsistent measurement standards across channels; and the large number and variety of vendors, which can make tool selection difficult. Then there's the complexity of accurately assessing return on investment in digital advertising; and on top of that, an overall lack of budget and resources to allocate to these efforts.

As well as the more specific ad tech tools, standard website traffic reporting tools like Google Analytics can provide many of the basic metrics for your activity, such as visitor numbers, bounce rates, conversions, video views and so on.

Whilst not all of these will be directly relevant to measuring your advertising activity, they can give you a more rounded view of how other areas of a website are performing.

Metrics that prioritize clicks and impressions are often used in digital marketing as a way of charging for and measuring the performance of digital advertising... but unsurprisingly, many are calling for a change.

These fairly simplistic metrics are based on traditional print advertising and early web standards that actually bear little comparison to today's online environment. They don't even give any indication of actual value to the advertiser, as there's no guarantee that a click-through will actually lead to a sale, or any other specified action.

In an age where mobile devices are prevalent, where fast scrolling is the norm and attention spans are short, it's becoming increasingly important to evaluate the quality of content and the amount of time users spend consuming it, in order to measure the real business impact.

More than ever, the focus of your measurement needs to be on how users will consume content, and how they might go on to engage with it. This will tend to call for more sophisticated insights such as 'attention-based' metrics.

Ultimately, if you're not conducting the appropriate analysis, then you'll just be guessing when it comes to optimizing your strategy.

One of the biggest measurement challenges in the digital marketing space is attribution.

Imagine if the only advertising you did for your business was to run a single ad in one newspaper. You probably won't reach much of your target audience, but you'd have a pretty good idea of how they found out about you...

The more variants or types of messaging you put out, and the more channels and types of media you use - the greater the chance of reaching your target audience, but... the harder it becomes to understand how a visitor came to do business with you.

On top of this, it's fairly unlikely that the first time they interact with your business is when they make that decision to 'convert'.

So, this presents a clear problem: how do you know which channel, or combination of channels, contributed to a user's decision to do business with you? Which is to say... which of them ultimately delivered a return on investment?

Advertising can play a major role throughout the customer journey, but in particular at the early stages: boosting initial awareness - especially if they're appearing to the right person, in the right place and in the right moment.

But it's generally less likely to be directly responsible for a new customer, where a visitor arrives at the site by clicking on the ad and immediately completes a purchase, or other action. On the other hand, if a visitor has already been made aware of the product - from an email newsletter, a recommendation from a friend or even from having seen the ad before -

serving them a retargeted ad could be just the push they need to make their decision.

Web analytics tools can be used to give you a more complete picture of the customer journey, from the very last thing a user clicked on immediately before making a purchase, to the online sources of any visits they've made to the site, prior to purchase. So, if they made a purchase immediately after clicking an ad, does the credit go to that ad, or to any of the touchpoints they interacted with along the way?

This is where attribution modelling comes in. Marketers decide on an attribution model, in which the various channels that played a role in a purchase decision are given - or 'attributed' with - varying levels of credit. The simplest forms of attribution modelling assign either first click credit, in which the channel that initially brought the visitor to the site gets all the credit, or last click, in which all credit goes to the last channel that ultimately led the customer to make a purchase.

Attribution modelling can be more nuanced than these approaches, in a linear model for example, all channels are assigned equal value... So, an ad that was part of a five-visit sequence, might be assigned 20% of the purchase credit, whereas an ad that led to only one of two visits before the transaction, might be worth 50%.

There really is no right or wrong answer about which attribution model is best for your business, and you should even consider using a few at a time, for a fuller view of your customers' journeys. Increasingly, however, advertisers are calling for more sophisticated multi-touch modelling software, which would allow them to assign credit to different channels and at different times.

Whilst mobile-specific platforms and channels will factor in to standard attribution, mobile advertisers sometimes need even more in-depth insights into which platforms and apps are the most effective for their messaging.

The goals of advertising in this context are many, from making users initially aware of apps and motivating them to download and install them, to placing ads within apps and measuring click throughs and engagement - all of which leads to a lot of potentially valuable insights.

Unlike web pages, however, there are no standards for app tracking, and even the Apple App Store and the Google Play Store have quite different rules.

With improvements already underway and new developments in modelling, analysis and reporting tools on the horizon, advertisers are getting a clearer idea of how their ads are performing - across a vast range of channels, platforms and devices.

What's most important for now though is having an understanding of the types of metrics that could be most helpful to your activities.

2. Ad Tech explained

Last chapter we covered the basics of the digital advertising 'ecosystem', exploring who's involved, how campaigns are planned, and the all-important issues of measurement and optimization.

This time we'll dig deeper into the technology itself, examining: the essential components of the 'ad stack'; a close examination of programmatic trading and some of the more sophisticated opportunities on offer today; before addressing some important issues in ad tech that you need to be aware of..

2.1. The ad stack

In conversations about ad tech, you'll often encounter the term 'ad stack', which is just a convenient way of referring to the various technologies and services that come together to serve a relevant ad to a targeted user, in the best place and at the best time.

As we'll see, there are various bits of tech used by different parties, and some that are used by all players involved.

We've already been introduced to the advertisers and publishers - the demand side and the supply side of the market, and they each have specific tools that help them with their activities...

Demand Side Platforms, or DSPs, help advertisers to buy and optimize ad placements. With so many options on offer, provided by so many different ad networks, exchanges and other inventory sources... it could all easily become a little too much. Thankfully, Demand Side Platforms allow advertisers to deal with all this on a single interface.

These platforms can also take on a lot of the work, allowing advertisers to automate the selection of inventory to meet certain criteria. The demographics and behaviors of the advertiser's desired audiences, the impressions they want to achieve and the price that they're willing to pay for them, and a blacklist of any publishers that the advertiser wants to steer clear of, are all taken into account. Some DSPs can also offer the ability to handle the management of ads both through direct deals with publishers and real-time bidding.

So, Demand Side Platforms help advertisers buy ad placements from multiple sources, in real time and via a single interface. Well, publishers are supported by a very similar platform... a Supply Side Platform, or SSP, which helps them to sell their inventory to many different advertisers, again: in real time, via a single interface.

Supply Side Platforms allow for the integration of pre-arranged deals and open ad exchanges, and for the setting of minimum bid levels, maximizing the potential for space to be used profitably. They also offer analysis and distribution of data about user characteristics to facilitate more informed ad buying, and ensure that the ads displayed are in line with the publisher's brand identity and values... and that the advertisers aren't undesirable or blacklisted for any reason.

DSPs and SSPs are the key technologies used by advertisers and publishers respectively, but - there's also a third party that complements their arrangement, providing valuable information that really lets the demand and the supply side make the most out of the opportunities on offer. These are data providers.

Effective digital advertising campaigns increasingly rely on huge volumes of data for accurate targeting, user segmenting, and personalization of creative in real time.

Data providers supply this data, and they do so using another component of the ad stack...

They use a Data Management Platform, or DMP - a unifying system that allows for the collection, integration, storage and analysis of data from multiple sources. This includes both first party data owned by the advertiser or publisher, and third-party data that's obtained elsewhere. Data Management Platforms primarily store user data and contextual data. User data includes demographic information like age, gender, marital status, income and geographic location. It also draws from historical information about past purchases, and predictive insights regarding levels of purchase intent.

Contextual data, on the other hand, gives a picture not of the user, but of the actual setting in which an ad might be displayed, and the content that might surround it. Also known as "semantic" data, this is an important extra layer of information.

Imagine that a publisher is selling ad space next to an article that discusses "sunbathing". Now, if you were a travel industry advertiser, wouldn't you want to know whether the article detailed the "best beaches in Florida", or "the biggest dangers of overexposure to the sun"?

DMP analysis can be used to estimate the audience numbers for an ad targeted to a particular user segment, or the potential response rate to a particular ad, so they can be very helpful to both advertisers and publishers in terms of maximizing the available opportunities.

There's an essential part of the ad stack that we haven't discussed yet: ad servers.

These are used across the digital advertising landscape by advertisers, agencies, publishers and ad networks alike to manage and run campaigns, typically making instantaneous decisions about which ads to display.

Ad servers can host a variety of display ad formats, and actually deliver the appropriate creative to visitors on publishers' sites and within mobile apps. They provide analytics such as tracking impressions and clicks for each ad and each publisher, allowing advertisers to monitor the performance of individual campaigns, and to compare their server's results with those reported by the vendors.

Some ad servers also have the capability to report on engagement metrics and conversions.

One of the best-known ad servers was DoubleClick, which became the industry leader following its acquisition by Google in 2008. This has since become part of the company's new platform known as Google Ad Manager - providing one integrated solution for all parties involved in the process.

Regardless of which ad server you're using… how does it 'know what to do'…?

An 'ad tag' is a piece of code, and the best way to explain them is probably by explaining how they're used...

Browsers use them to request either an ad or another tag from an ad server. Advertisers use them to direct the user's browser to load a specific creative. Publishers use them to sell ad space. Ad servers use them to control decision-making about which ads to show

… and Data Providers use them to collect information about users for segmentation and personalization purposes.

So, here's how the process works, step by step, for a publisher…

1.   When a user calls up a publisher's site or mobile app, the browser sends an initial ad tag to the ad server for that publisher. This tag contains information about the user and about the size of the ad placement.

2.   The publisher's ad server may, in turn, send another ad tag to a data provider to access any relevant information about contextual targeting or personalization.

3.   The ad server then passes a tag to the advertiser to obtain an ad. This may either be a direct request for a pre-existing guaranteed buy, or it might request bids from multiple advertisers and conduct an auction to achieve the most profitable real-time deal for the publisher.

4.   The ad server then delivers a final ad tag to the user's browser… which contains a link for the creative to be displayed.

So that's an overview of how different components of the ad stack work together to ensure that an ad appears - at least in theory - to the right user, in the right place and at the right time.

2.2.   Trading and personalization

Now that we're familiar with the key components of the 'ad stack', it's time to look in more detail at how ad tech facilitates 'programmatic trading' - the automated buying and selling of ads in real-time.

It's important to recognize that many companies will contract out the management of their ad trading to external agencies that carry out programmatic and other media buying for them. To facilitate this, the agency may layer their own platform on top of the DSP or other ad tech that the client is running.

Agency trading desks perform tasks such as ad verification, dynamic creative optimization, and audience measurement and reporting.

Private trading desks, also known as 'Programmatic Buying Units', are agency teams that are exclusively dedicated to media buying, optimization and reporting for just one client.

There are enormous amounts of online advertising opportunities, some targeting niche audiences, and some for more general viewership. This leads to hugely complex tasks in managing multiple campaigns and target audiences, together with ensuring that the right creative runs in the right ad slots, and making appropriate payments...

Ad networks can help in this area by acting as a middleman, directing advertisers to a wide range of publishers with available inventory that meets their marketing needs, particularly "remnant" placements that haven't already been directly sold.

Inventory is typically sold in categories such as "males aged 25-34", "movie sites", or by specific site or page.

Ad network services can connect with both DSPs and SSPs.

Because it's important for networks to maintain transparency around their processes, they rely on robust analytics and reporting tools for accurate tracking of impressions, as well as accounting software that can ensure on-time payments and deal with international currency transfers.

On ad exchanges, advertisers bid for publishers' available inventory in real time. The ad exchange is an autonomous auction-driven platform that facilitates programmatic ad buying, and so is used by all players in the digital advertising space, including ad networks which buy unused inventory to mark up and sell for a profit.

Programmatic trading employs sophisticated algorithms to ensure that advertisers and publishers can both achieve optimal results.

Open ad exchanges, as they sound, are public marketplaces with inventory from many publishers that's available to anyone. These exchanges are attractive to brands looking for the widest range of publicity, but offer a much lower level of information and control over which publishers are used, and have led to widespread concerns about ad fraud.

Individual publishers are establishing private marketplaces in which they invite known advertisers to participate in the auction, but on pre-agreed terms with regards to target audience, type of inventory, ad formats, frequency caps - which control the number of times an ad can be shown to each user - and so on. Private marketplaces can ban selected ad networks or other vendors, and are generally considered to be more secure and transparent.

On pay per click and social media advertising platforms, bids are generally set either manually or automatically. Manual bidding allows advertisers to define a cap on the amount that they're willing to pay, whereas automatic bidding specifies that ads will be shown at the lowest possible cost, but the actual price will be determined by the system, with no cap.

In this scenario, manual bidding offers more control and the opportunity to optimize the use of the available budget. However, automated bidding has the advantage of being low maintenance, especially for large campaigns.

When ads are traded programmatically, 'real-time bidding' allows for the live trading of individual ad impressions in the form of an auction, typically via an ad exchange...

1.   SSPs list their inventory on the ad exchange, with full details of page location, topics, and so on...

2.   When a user enters the address of a publisher's site - meaning that a page needs to be generated for viewing - available impressions for that page automatically appear in the auction.

3.   Data about the user is collected and sent to the publisher's server and to the ad exchange.

4.   The ad exchange sends bid requests to DSPs and to ad networks. Each DSP reviews the impression opportunity and all relevant information about the user and the placement to decide whether to bid. If so, it sends its maximum price offer and the location of the ad creative back to the ad exchange.

5.   The ad exchange reviews all the bids that it receives for the impression, and eliminates any that do not meet the requirements of the publisher. For example, the publisher may have specified that it only wants ads in a certain language, or around a specific topic.

6.   The ad exchange then sells the impression to the highest remaining bidder. The 'winning' ad is served in the page displayed to the user.

This entire process takes place in milliseconds... just before the ad is delivered, with millions of impressions being handled at the same time, without impacting the load speed of the page, and without the user even being aware of what's happening!

'Header bidding' is an advanced programmatic technique whereby advertisers get priority "pre-bid" looks at inventory across a number of ad exchanges simultaneously...

Competing in real time for specific impressions, rather than being part of the general auction, offers benefits for both sides. Advertisers gain from being able to see and bid on a wide range of inventory, while publishers benefit from the greater exposure.

A publisher puts a piece of code into the header section of their web page - containing a list of advertisers to be contacted if inventory becomes available.

When the page is requested by a user, the code fires and invites bids from those advertisers for all of the placements and formats that are currently open. The publisher's server receives the responses, allocates impressions to the highest bidder, and the page is loaded and displayed to the user.

One unforeseen consequence of header bidding has been that DSPs are inundated with bid requests – often far more than their infrastructure can cope with.

Since ad exchanges can be included in the header lists, bid requests for the same impression can be duplicated, causing confusion about the source of the request.

Supply Path Optimization refers to the methods that DSPs and agencies use to identify the bids that are most likely to win in an auction. These methods employ algorithms to purge duplicate or suspect bid requests and to prioritize those that each advertiser is most likely to win.

Publishers can also use supply path optimization to reverse engineer this process and identify ways to optimize how their inventory reaches buyers.

Overall, both the demand and supply side of digital advertising are looking to increase quality and transparency and to reduce the need for middlemen in their transactions.

Aside from the sophisticated tools and methods now available for automating the process of trading ads, continued developments in ad tech now allow for users to enjoy an extremely personalized advertising experience...

As with many marketing tactics, the use of personalization to engage individual users can significantly improve campaign results.

A technique known as 'Dynamic Creative Optimization' allows advertisers to customize ads in real time using parameters such as gender, age, known behaviors and preferences, purchase history... and can even factor in location, time of day and prevailing weather conditions.

So, for example, a coffee lover in Chicago during the winter might be offered a coupon for a hot mocha, whereas someone in Arizona at the same time might be notified of iced coffee specials. Another person in Arizona who's never purchased a coffee might receive a promotion for a new smoothie flavor.

Of course, to do this effectively requires both vast amounts of - hopefully accurate - data and also... potentially hundreds or even thousands of variations of a given ad. Specialist companies can handle serving the appropriate creative and layering on rich media, dynamic messaging and features such as customized maps or videos.

The possible graphical components of each ad are defined when the campaign is set up, and, rather than showing the same ad to every viewer, the optimal dynamic content is determined in real time as the ad is served to each individual, including both the actual components shown and the creative look and feel, such as color choice and the wording of any 'calls to action'. In fact, machine learning is now used to study the results and help to continuously refine the process.

The availability of this technique means that the initial design and definition of a campaign can be much simpler, since the creative staff can be less concerned with ways to appeal to specific target audiences. Instead, they're free to focus on imaginative visuals and content, while the Dynamic Creative Optimization manages data analysis and ad delivery.

Often, it's not enough to simply identify a user and serve them a single ad.

Ad retargeting refers to the practice of showing users ads based on their previous interactions with a company's digital presence, especially for those users who might have initiated some level of conversion such as a purchase or filling in an enquiry form, but who failed to complete it.

Retargeting works by dropping a cookie from the advertiser's site onto the user's browser. This can be checked for by publisher sites, ensuring that retargeted ads are only shown to users who are already somewhat familiar with the business.

Retargeting solutions may be included in a comprehensive advertising platform, or they may be stand-alone, with the ability to integrate with other tools. Sophisticated retargeting systems can perform audience targeting and segmentation, oversee automated bidding and manage creative, as well as providing detailed analysis and reporting.

3. Ad verification

Global spending on digital advertising now easily surpasses $300 billion... and marketers believe that a massive 30% of that spend is actually wasted.

Whilst some of that wastage can be attributed to marketers' own strategies or choice of channels, significant amounts are actually lost due to ads that, for various reasons, aren't seen by the right users - if they're even seen by users at all.

Ad verification aims to verify where ads are being served in order to reduce this wasted spend, and to protect both advertisers and publishers against any damage that could be caused by misplaced advertising.

In this chapter, we'll explore exactly how all this works, before going in-depth into the three key areas that ad verification tools address: ad viewability, ad fraud, and brand safety.

3.1. Ad verification and viewability

The term 'ad verification' refers to the techniques that allow marketers to check that their ads are appearing in appropriate places online, that they're positioned correctly, and that they can be seen by their target audiences.

Essentially, it makes sure ads are appearing where and how they're meant to.

Here, we should point out that ad verification is rarely a concern of users themselves. Verification only takes place after an ad has been served – it doesn't actively stop ads from appearing in the wrong place, but rather highlights when they do.

As such, ad verification is extremely important to both advertisers and publishers. Understanding and addressing the insights provided by ad verification tools can help advertisers avoid wasted ad spend; whilst publishers can avoid paying for fraudulent traffic, and displaying inappropriate, malicious, or even illegal ads.

These issues are especially prevalent given the rise of programmatic trading – the digital, automated buying and selling of inventory.

Due to its automation, it can be hard to guarantee where programmatically-traded ads end up. For example, a huge number of ads are shown on fraudulent sites, fail to reach the desired viewers, or just don't display correctly in users' browsers.

By gaining a better understanding of where these ads are going, both advertisers and publishers can take steps to prevent, and protect themselves from wasted spend and damaged reputations.

Clearly, ad verification is important. So, how does it work?

Ad verification tools are an important part of the ad tech world. They aim to check that an ad has been served according to the terms that were agreed upon by both the advertiser and the publisher.

In the context of programmatic trading, ad verification tools track ad impressions, which are reported each time an individual ad is served to a user on a page.

In order to do this, an ad verification tag is included within the code, or the 'ad schema markup', to be precise. When an ad request is triggered, the ad - including the verification tag - is sent to the ad server - the piece of technology that actually inserts the ad into a page. The ad is then served, generating an impression.

Once the impression has been served, this tag can then analyze the publisher's page to ensure that it's appropriately placed, before reporting back to both the advertiser, as well as the publisher and the ad exchange - the programmatic marketplace which facilitated the agreement between the advertiser and publisher.

Sometimes, the verification tool that does this will be integrated within the demand- side platform, or DSP - the platform responsible for helping the advertiser buy and optimize ad placements. However, more often, ad verification tools are operated by vendors entirely separate from the demand side. This is because third party verification vendors can often provide a more objective and independent determination on whether an ad impression was served according to agreed-upon criteria.

At this point, we've covered what ad verification is, why it's important, and how it works. Now it's time to dive a little deeper.

In particular, ad verification tackles three major issues within the digital advertising world: viewability, or whether an impression is viewable on a user's screen; ad fraud – whether an impression is requested by and served to human users within the defined target market for the campaign; and finally, brand safety, or whether the impression is served in an appropriate and brand-friendly context.

Let's start by looking at viewability.

'Viewability' is the measurement of how much of an ad appears on a user's screen, and for how long. In other words, it's the determination of whether an ad has had the chance to be seen by the user it was served to.

It should almost go without saying, but this is incredibly important for advertisers - if their ad can't be seen, it's not going to have much of an impact.

It's important to note that viewability tools can't tell us whether a user actually saw an ad. Rather, they can help answer the question: did an ad have the opportunity to be seen?

But what does this mean in practice?

The global industry standard as set out by the Internet Advertising Bureau and the Media Rating Council states that a display ad impression is only viewable if at least half of its pixels are on the user's screen for at least one second; or for video ads, at least half of the video player must be on screen for at least two seconds.

So, if a user clicks on a webpage – causing an ad to be served – but scrolls past that ad before it fully loads, that impression would not meet these viewability standards. Or, if there's an ad at the very bottom of the page they're viewing, but they never scroll down far enough for it to be on screen, that ad impression would also not be viewable.

If you think that a standard of half an ad impression on screen for one or two seconds doesn't sound like much, well... you're not alone. A recent survey of senior marketers carried out by the CMO Council found that more than 40% of respondents disagree with these standards.

In fact, some advertisers are even imposing their own rules for viewability. For example, IBM requires 100% of a display ad impression to be on screen for a minimum of two seconds for it to be viewable; and for video impressions, 100% of the video player must be in view for at least half of its total duration time. However, there is no clear consensus on the best standard for viewability, so for now, the IAB and MRC's industry standards remain in place.

Clearly viewability is important for advertisers - in fact, some are opting for a pricing model which means they are only charged for impressions which are measured as viewable.

The standard pricing model in advertising is CPM, or 'cost per mille'. Here, an advertiser pays a set price for one thousand impressions, regardless of whether or not those impressions were actually viewable. This means advertisers might pay for 1,000 impressions when, in reality, only 500 of them even had the chance to be seen.

Given that, according to insights from Google, more than 50% of ads aren't viewable, this isn't ideal. This has led some to opt for vCPM or 'viewable cost per mille'. With this model, advertisers pay a set price for one thousand impressions that meet standards for viewability, even if that means serving significantly more impressions to get to that number. This is known as 'guaranteed viewability'.

When opting for vCPM, it's important for advertisers to understand how the publishers they work with are defining viewability. As we've seen, standards vary and, without checking, advertisers could end up paying for a lower standard of viewability than they were expecting.

This can be especially costly considering that guaranteed viewability does often come at a higher premium. Alongside understanding what you're paying for, it's also important to find a balance that meets the needs and budget of a campaign.

So, we've covered what viewability is and what constitutes a viewable impression. But how can viewability rates be improved?

Viewability rates vary according to region and by industry, with popular content categories such as games and music having higher viewability rates for both video and display ads, presumably because users tend to engage with these more and therefore keep them on screen for longer. For all formats, viewability rates for mobile devices and tablets are consistently higher than on desktops.

As we've said, there are a number of factors that can impact ad viewability, and not all of them will be within your control. However, there are some ways in which both advertisers and publishers can improve the chances of an ad being seen.

Let's take a look at some of those methods, starting with steps advertisers can take.

When it comes to increasing viewability, one of the most important elements to consider is the ad formats you'll use.

Certain ad formats can massively improve your viewability rates. Take native in-app advertising. This type of advertising should only load when in-view — which isn't necessarily true of advertising on desktop or mobile web browsers. Because of this, this type of advertising should come hand-in-hand with high viewability rates.

However, it's important to bear in mind that ad format decisions should be about more than just viewability.

Let's take a look at sticky ads. Available on both desktop and mobile devices, sticky ads occupy a fixed place on a user's screen as they scroll through content. This means they often come with incredibly high viewability rates, since they are always on screen.

But… sticky ads are also considered incredibly intrusive by users, as they can block the content, they're actually on the page to see. This has even led some browsers and publishers to block this type of advertising - they might come with high viewability rates… but they do so at a cost.

So, when choosing the ad formats, you want to opt for, you need to find a careful balance between ads that are viewable and ads that provide the best advertising experience.

The ad formats advertisers use can have a huge effect on viewability rates, but of course, it isn't the only element you need to consider. Advertisers shouldn't underestimate the impact that ad sizing, page placement, responsive design and channel placement can all have on viewability…

Clearly, there are a lot of elements advertisers should consider when it comes to increasing the viewability of advertising. But what can publishers do to increase the viewability of their offerings?

Well, firstly, there's page loading speed. Slow loading pages can annoy users, who can lose patience and leave a page before any ads have even loaded. Ensuring a page's content and advertising load quickly should generate more viewable impressions - and make for a better user experience over all.

In the same way, page length should also be a consideration. Users often don't want to scroll through multiple or long pages. If you host advertising at the bottom of a long page, or on the second or third page of content, it's likely that a user won't scroll that far to see it, meaning that the advertising found there won't be viewable. Instead, shorter, one-page content tends to generate the highest viewability rates.

And finally, there's page design. Publishers should aim to keep the layout of their pages simple. Advertisers want their advertising to be seen, and it's likely that their ads will get missed if there are too many competing elements. Tools may still verify ads as meeting viewability standards even on a busy page, but keeping a page simple will increase the likelihood that a user will actually see an ad.

So, ad verification tools are used to check that an ad impression has been served according to the terms that were agreed upon by the advertiser and the publisher. As we've discussed, one area that these provide insight into is viewability, and there are a number of steps that both advertisers and publishers can take to increase the chances of an ad being seen.

3.2.   Ad fraud and Brand safety

So far, we've looked at what ad verification is, and how it concerns viewability. In this chapter, we'll explore the two other key areas verification tools address: ad fraud and brand safety.

Ad fraud is the practice of deliberately manipulating ad serving systems to generate illegitimate income. Advertisers are typically the victims of this activity - for example, fraudsters might deceive them into paying by overstating the number of impressions an ad received, misrepresenting ad inventory, or generating fake click throughs.

Publishers can also be victims of ad fraud. Many publishers pay for some traffic in order to satisfy their page view number guarantees, and these transactions can be exploited. Or, publishers can even be tricked into displaying illegal or malicious ads.

It's difficult to calculate the true cost of ad fraud - recent estimates vary from $6.5 billion to as high as $19 billion annually - but there's no question that huge amounts of money are involved.

Ad fraud schemes can be massive. A recent international scheme involved 125 Android apps, which were acquired by a network of shell companies based in a number of different countries. More than 115 million users who downloaded these apps were secretly tracked, and their behavior was then used to program a huge network of computers that could mimic human activity and thus avoid fraud detection systems. And, to avoid suspicion, the shell owners continued to maintain the apps to keep real users engaged and to have sufficient cover for the fake traffic.

Not all schemes will look like this. Perpetrators of ad fraud can range from individuals or small groups looking to make some quick money; to large, well-organized criminal enterprises.

For the most part, fraudsters tend to be attracted to newer technologies where the ad tech markets are less mature, and the systems to detect fraud haven't yet developed sufficiently robust methodologies - technologies like mobile web browsers and apps, or video and internet-connected TV.

To get a better idea of the different forms ad fraud can take, let's explore some of the most common tactics...

To be able to protect yourself against ad fraud, it's important to be aware of the different forms it can take...

One of the most common techniques is the use of a botnet. Bots are programs that can perform typical user actions such as clicking on links; and can even have simulated user profiles, which then enables them to be segmented and targeted. When groups of these bots hosted on multiple computers work together, they form a botnet, where these activities can be done at scale.

Then, there's ghost sites. These are real websites with actual content - however, this content is often low-quality or stolen. These sites only exist to create more ad inventory that can be sold to advertisers, and often, botnets are responsible for the traffic or impressions reported.

Alongside this, there's domain spoofing. This is when ad inventory from low-quality sites is listed as belonging to more established or reputable publishers. As a result, advertisers may believe they are purchasing quality placements when, in reality, they are paying for substandard inventory.

Another commonly used ad fraud method is pixel stuffing. Here, an ad spot is placed in a 1x1 pixel so that, when an ad is served, an impression is reported, but the ad is too small to actually be seen on the page.

Next, there's ad stacking. This is where ads are displayed in a layer so that only the top ad is visible, but all the ads in the stack report an impression. In some cases, fraudsters even generate clicks on the ads and download links beneath the top ad so that it appears that actual users took these actions, whereas in reality, real users had no knowledge of them.

And finally, there's ad injection. Here, ads are inserted into a page without the permission of the publisher, or the ad that should be displayed is replaced by an illegitimate one.

Of course, ad fraud techniques aren't limited to only these, and popular tactics change as fraud prevention evolves. Staying aware of how ad fraud techniques are changing can make all the difference in keeping the digital ecosystem a safe environment for advertising.

So, we've established that ad fraud can be costly to both advertisers and publishers, and explored some of the most common tactics being used by fraudsters.

But what can be done to protect your company against fraud?

First and foremost, it's important to recognize when you've fallen victim to fraudulent activity. Generally, it's not possible to identify that fraudulent activity has occurred until after an ad has been delivered, and the campaign results are evaluated. This means it's vital to keep an eye on campaign data. Signs that a business may have been exposed to fraud include a campaign significantly underperforming, or reported metrics that seem 'too good to be true' - results like 100% viewability or no suspect impressions at all. If a result seems too good to be true, it probably is...

Sometimes, signs of ad fraud can fly under the radar. For this reason, it's typically worthwhile to work with a third-party ad fraud partner, who can help your company detect fraudulent activity, and implement steps to prevent it.

Some of the measures you take will be dependent on the type of fraud you've fallen victim to. For example, one option in the case of click fraud - in which you suspect that fake clicks are being generated - is to move away from paying for clicks, and instead only pay for conversions - that is, only paying when a user has completed the desired action or end result, like making a purchase, signing up for a mailing list, or downloading an app.

But beyond being aware of specific types of ad fraud, both advertisers and publishers should follow industry-wide initiatives.

One example is the IAB Tech Lab's ads.txt initiative - a practice that's already been adopted by approximately three-quarters of publishers, according to eMarketer.

Here, publishers are encouraged to place a file called ads.txt on their domains which lists the parties that are authorized to sell their inventory. This then allows advertisers to check that they're buying placements from a legitimate source.

The file should be very easy to create and maintain, and since it can only be uploaded by the owner of the publisher domain, it's relatively secure. However, this practice is not foolproof - in late 2018, a scam was identified which actually exploited ads.txt. This doesn't mean that you shouldn't use it, only it should be used in tandem with other fraud protection tactics.

Another industry initiative you should be aware of is the certification program launched by the Trustworthy Accountability Group, or TAG. This provides a set of guidelines to prevent fraud, with requirements that vary depending on a company's role in the digital advertising ecosystem.

Companies that meet these standards receive a "Certified Against Fraud" seal, and gain access to a set of reporting tools that can help in preventing fraudulent activity. This includes a Payment ID system, which allows advertisers to ensure their payments are made to legitimate vendors; a Data Centre IP list, an up-to-date list containing IP addresses of invalid data centers that companies should avoid; and Publisher Sourcing Disclosure Requirements, a policy under which publishers disclose their levels of verified traffic.

Following industry guidelines is a vital step in fighting ad fraud. However, it continues to be a significant issue, and advertisers and publishers need to ensure that they use credible third-party verification and remain vigilant.

Of course, ad fraud isn't the only issue affecting the safety of the advertising ecosystem. One of the most pressing issues that ad verification tools aim to tackle is brand safety.

Brand safety refers to the potential for an ad to appear in relation to content that is offensive or inappropriate, and is therefore detrimental to a brand's image, mission or goals. The definition of what constitutes offensive or inappropriate content is pretty subjective - some brands are even wary of advertising on news pages that cover politically-charged topics.

Protecting brand safety is a key issue for both advertisers and publishers - one poorly placed ad can severely impact a brand's reputation - whether that's just the opinion of the user that the ad was served to, or even on a much wider scale…

It's hardly surprising that so many digital advertising professionals view brand safety as a major concern. In fact, according to eMarketer, some consider brand safety to be one of the top three issues currently posing the greatest threat to their marketing success, after changing consumer expectations and the actual loss of customers.

And this issue isn't getting any simpler. As the digital advertising ecosystem develops - and the amount of content and platforms available to marketers grow - the issue of protecting brand safety is becoming increasingly complex.

The technology behind monitoring brand safety is having to evolve to keep up with this growing complexity, especially as advertisers demand more in the way of transparency and trust.

To date, the use of keywords has been a common means of determining 'safe' content. However, this now isn't enough - given the huge amount of content online.

Online news and current affairs provide an excellent illustration of this issue. Often rife with controversial, negative or upsetting content, when advertisers run searches for banned keywords and terms on breaking news and tabloid sites, it's hardly surprising that they encounter multiple red flags. Indeed, these factual reports are often automatically avoided, as relatively common words such as 'death', 'crash' or 'fight' are guaranteed to set off sensors.

It's difficult to identify the full range of specific words that should flag content to be avoided. Not only this, but there's also a high risk of false positives - words that incorrectly flag some placements as unsafe, resulting in a loss of potentially valuable advertising opportunities.

As a result, safe pages, or even entire websites, where the context is lost due to a keyword-only approach are blocked.

As such, natural language processing and artificial intelligence are now being incorporated into developing tools for protecting brand safety. These technologies can interpret linguistic subtleties where the exact meaning of words can change depending on the context and are capable of analyzing every page on a publisher site to pinpoint appropriate placements at a granular level.

Not everyone is convinced that these algorithms are yet sophisticated enough to allow brands to rely on a fully automated system. Human input is still required to ensure specific brand standards are included within the programs, and to build whitelists and blacklists which detail which publishers should and shouldn't be worked with.

So, that's it for our look at ad verification, in which we explored viewability, ad fraud and brand safety. As with many of the ad tech practices, we may be accustomed with, it's likely that the nature and methods of ad verification will evolve as the digital ecosystem grows and changes. Keeping up with developments in this area is vital in protecting the spend - and safety - of advertisers and publishers.

Ad Tech and Programmatic

Part II

Programmatic

4. Understanding programmatic

Programmatic's a pretty big topic in the marketing world, and it's likely that you'll at least have heard it mentioned before - but what does 'programmatic' really mean, and how has it evolved over time?

These chapters will give you a solid understanding of how and why programmatic has become such an integral part of the way ads are bought, sold and targeted.

4.1. The evolution of Programmatic

First things first: what does the term programmatic actually mean? It can seem complicated, but really programmatic is just a word for the automated buying and selling of media space. In other words, it's just another way of trading ads, using technology and automated bidding processes rather than going directly to the media owner and brokering a deal. Programmatic trading is used to make the buying and selling of ad inventory more efficient for all parties involved, because it cuts out the lengthy negotiations between advertisers, media agencies and media owners.

So that's what programmatic actually is. What sometimes confuses people is the technology that makes programmatic work. There are various technological components that work together to make programmatic trading possible, and they didn't all arrive on the scene at the same time. The advertising landscape used to look very different to the one we've got now. To explain how it all came about, we're going to take you back to a time before programmatic existed at all…

Media owners need to sell as much of their ad inventory as possible in order to make their sites profitable. Typically, their inventory can be broadly divided into two categories: premium inventory, which sits on the site or section home pages and is seen by lots of users, and remnant inventory which is located on the less frequently visited pages of the site, or in less prominent positions on a page, and so in the past these ad spots tended to command a pretty low value, or even went unsold.

However, this remnant inventory accounts for the vast majority of total ad impressions on a site – so, when bought in bulk, it's actually of significant value to advertisers and media agencies. Media owners recognized this, so they banded together to form ad networks: basically, just groups of sites who packaged up and sold their remnant inventory in bundles.

This helped for a while, since buyers were able to buy scaled propositions much more easily than before. However, soon there were so many ad networks in the market that buyers found themselves struggling to figure out which one to turn to for the best inventory at the best price. They realized they needed a way to identify and purchase the right inventory – one that didn't involve a team of people sitting at screens, contacting media owner after media owner looking for the best deal. And media owners realized they needed a method of communicating their available inventory to as many potential buyers as possible, maximizing the price of their impressions without the need to negotiate with the ad networks. These requirements formed the foundation of the programmatic trading model that exists today.

In its simplest form, programmatic trading requires three pieces of technology. Bear in mind that these 'pieces of technology' aren't physical objects - they're just pieces of software. DSPs (or demand-side platforms) are used by the buyers – media agencies or advertisers – who have a demand for ad inventory. DSPs hold information from the buy- side about criteria for the ad inventory they need – target audience and maximum bid price, among other data.

On the other side, SSPs (or supply-side platforms) are used by the sellers – media owners – who are supplying ad inventory. SSPs hold a record of the inventory a media owner wants to sell, the different audience segments that visit the media owner's site, and the minimum price the media owner wants to sell for.

And in the middle of DSPs and SSPs sits the ad exchange: the piece of technology which auctions off the ad inventory made available by the SSPs. Buyers will be entered in for an auction if the inventory available matches the criteria in their DSP – and then the one with the highest maximum bid price will win.

Often, you'll hear a company being referred to as a DSP, SSP, or an ad exchange. This just means that that company provides that kind of software - so, for example, the company DataXu will often be referred to as a DSP, because that's what they do.

This might sound like a long process – but it actually all happens in a fraction of a second. The auction process starts when a user opens a page with an ad unit on it, and the ad that wins the auction appears at the same time that the rest of the page loads – so it's pretty quick! This process is often referred to as real-time bidding, or RTB.

Because the ads are delivered to users in real-time, programmatic allows buyers to make use of data. Gone are the days of buying inventory on a media owner's site in the hope that it'd reach your target audience – now you can set rules in your DSP to make sure you're only entered into auctions when an ad request is triggered by a user who matches your target criteria. For example, if you drop a cookie on a user who puts a product on your site into their shopping cart but doesn't make a purchase, you can choose to retarget them with relevant messages whenever they encounter an ad spot that's available for you to bid on. Or, if you want to target adults in their mid-20s who like to travel, you can do that too. The main thing to realize is that RTB works by trading against an audience - you specify the audience who should see your ad, and bid on that audience.

When you think about all the different targeting criteria a buyer might want to bid on, you start to realize just how vast these data sets really are. Media owners will use this data to segment their audience, dividing them up into smaller audiences according to characteristics like gender, age, behavior or interest. These segments are then made available through SSPs... but imagine if it was the job of just one person to identify every possible cross-section of an audience that buyers might want to target! That's why a lot

of media owners now use data management platforms, or DMPs — these help to segment and manage the huge amounts of data that media owners need to be able to make sense of in order to make the most of their inventory's value.

It's important to realize that when all of these technologies first came into play, they were only really built to facilitate programmatic trading for desktop. That's mainly because, when programmatic trading first started in 2007, mobile browsing was nowhere near as popular as it is today. Plus, mobile's technological ecosystem sat almost completely apart from desktop, and creative opportunities on mobile were extremely limited. All this put together meant that media owners focused heavily on developing their desktop propositions instead — so that's where the best opportunities for advertisers were found.

As mobile traffic grew over time though, buyers and sellers alike began to realize that there were significant opportunities in making programmatic trading available for mobile. This growth area created opportunities for some new players to enter the market, with fewer restrictions than the traditional players — and so new DSPs, ad exchanges and SSPs with a specific focus on mobile inventory emerged. However, as in most industries, many of the newer, smaller entrants were eventually acquired by pre-existing companies. For example: the mobile SSP Nexage was bought by the mobile ad network Millennial Media. Millennial Media was then bought by AOL who, in turn, were bought by Verizon in 2016. This simplified things for advertisers and media agencies who want to be able to turn to one company for all their media buying needs.

Mergers and acquisitions like these have meant that, for the most part, the buy side can now access mobile programmatic inventory through the same DSPs (connecting to the same ad exchanges) as desktop inventory. That allows most media agencies to take a 'device-agnostic' approach to media planning and buying, where the focus is on targeting and optimizing for the right audience, no matter which device they're on.

On the sell side, there are still some mobile focused SSPs out there, but these are mainly used by media owners who house most of their inventory within mobile apps. For media owners whose audience can be found across different devices, SSPs like AppNexus and Rubicon are among the most commonly used.

In the early days of programmatic trading the only inventory that was really bought and sold programmatically were standard display formats – think banners and MPUs. Buyers were only really comfortable purchasing ad spots programmatically if they knew exactly what the formats looked like, and could guarantee that their creative would work in the units they were paying for. That did put a certain limit on how creative advertisers were able to be when trading programmatically, though, so programmatic was mostly used for performance-driven campaigns, where optimizing for targeting and relevance is far more important than having the kind of unique creative needed for branding campaigns.

However, the advantages programmatic offers – a more streamlined buying process and the ability to use data to get the right message in front of the right person at the right time – attracted lots of media owners, agencies and advertisers who didn't want to focus on trading remnant standard display alone. Programmatic's advantages mean that it's no longer just remnant inventory being traded – there are plenty of media owners who trade all of their inventory in this way, and that proportion is only going to grow as time and technologies advance. On top of this, the programmatic market has now expanded to include much more than just display – it's now used in the buying and selling of ads in TV, radio, out of home and even print! We'll talk more about how programmatic works for each of these media channels later on.

This is a good time to mention something that you probably noticed was missing from that list: social formats. While social platforms often describe their method of selling ad inventory as 'programmatic' - because it's sold through an automated auction method using data for targeting purposes - this kind of 'programmatic' isn't quite the same as the one we've been talking about so far. That's because social platforms essentially exist outside of the ordinary programmatic landscape. You won't find any of their inventory on an ad exchange - if you want to buy an ad spot on Facebook, you'll go directly to Facebook's API and submit all your requirements there.

As you can see, programmatic is becoming more and more commonplace. In fact, these days if a media owner wants to make a direct sale, they usually have to offer something unique, like a content partnership. As programmatic continues to evolve, it's presenting media owners, media agencies and advertisers with new opportunities - and new challenges - all the time.

4.2.   Methods of Execution

So now you know about the basic technologies used in programmatic trading, and you've got an idea of the different media channels and devices where programmatic happens. What we haven't covered yet are the different trading methods used. There are multiple ways of selling inventory, and media owners can choose which one works best for them depending on who they want to sell to.

Advertisers might choose to make their inventory available on what's known as the open exchange, or open marketplace. You can think of this as making ad inventory available to the widest possible pool of buyers – whoever wants to can enter the open exchange and place a bid on the inventory available there. That means sellers can offer their inventory to a lot of buyers at once, while buyers can target their audience across a huge number of sites. Even if buyers aren't sure exactly which audience will perform best, the open exchange is a great place to try a 'test and learn' strategy, because it's where you'll find the largest variety of parameters you could optimize against. By casting the net wide and buying inventory across different devices, formats, publishers, locations or even times of day, you'll start to gather the data you need on where your best-performing audience can be found and, crucially, who they are.

Of course, with all this available inventory and demand on the open exchange it can sometimes be difficult to determine exactly who you're trading with. Advertisers and media agencies have found it notoriously difficult to track where their ads are ending up and whether that's on reputable sites, while media owners are wary of flooding their sites with low quality advertising. These issues have prompted publishers to keep much of their premium inventory away from the open exchange. However, buyers and sellers alike still want to benefit from the ease of trading that programmatic offers, so they've found ways to circumvent the issues of the open marketplace. Many of these more private ways of trading are done with the help of deal IDs.

A deal ID is a unique code that enables buyers and sellers to create direct relationships with one another within the programmatic ecosystem. Media owners can create as many deal IDs as they want, and each one is linked to a predefined type of inventory – whether that's refined by ad format, placement on the page, minimum bid price or anything else. They then share the deal IDs with their chosen buyers, who'll know what each deal ID relates to and therefore have a much clearer understanding of what they're buying. This basically allows buyers and sellers to operate in a controlled and closed environment that resembles direct sales, while still benefiting from the ease of programmatic trading.

One way of avoiding the issues of the open marketplace is for media owners to run private marketplaces, or PMPs.

PMPs allow media owners to restrict the pool of potential buyers, since buyers have to be granted entry into the private marketplace by the relevant media owner. Buyers will likely only enter into a private marketplace if they know exactly what they're buying and where, though, so it's also a good way for them to guarantee transparency. PMPs still stimulate competition, as they offer a specified inventory package to several buyers at the same time, forcing them to outbid one another if they want to win the auction. That helps media owners make sure they're getting the best price for their inventory.

For those who are looking for something even more exclusive, there's programmatic direct or programmatic guaranteed.

This is basically where buyers and sellers reach a one-to-one agreement. Before the sale is agreed, both sides will agree parameters including price, inventory volume, audience segments and so on. It works very much like a traditional direct sale, so there are no bidding wars here! That does mean that programmatic guaranteed is a pretty big departure from the other forms of programmatic we've talked about, since almost everything except the final sale will need to take the form of direct conversations between buyers and sellers. However, the setup, ad delivery, management and reporting can still be operated in the same way as any other programmatic campaign – so there's still an increase in efficiency, as well as improved options for analysis and optimization.

Media owners won't generally pick just one of these routes to sale, though. Historically, media owners have mostly opted for what's known as a 'waterfall' approach to trading inventory. It's called the waterfall model because impressions start at the 'top' where the media owners try to sell to the most desirable buyers, and then trickle down to the 'bottom' where the inventory is available to anyone who wants to bid.

This is done by setting a series of rules within the SSP that determine which methods should be used to sell an impression, and in which order. Usually media owners will start by trying to sell within the channels that have the smallest pool of potential buyers and the highest CPMs – so programmatic guaranteed. If the available impression doesn't fit the targeting criteria for any of the buyers in that pool, it'll be passed down to the media owner's private marketplaces. And if there are still no bids made by any of the DSPs, or if the bids are lower than the media owner's floor price, or minimum price a media owner is willing to sell for, the impression is passed on to the open exchange.

Although it may seem like inventory is bound to command the highest CPMs when sold via programmatic guaranteed or PMPs, that's actually not always the case. Sometimes there might be bidders on the open exchange who are willing to pay premium prices for a particular ad spot – because it might be exactly what they're looking for. The linear waterfall approach has also been known to result in 'lost' impressions, where an error occurs while the impression is being passed down the waterfall and it never ends up reaching the potential buyers. So, you can see why media owners started thinking it might be time to shake things up a little and switch their sales tactics away from the traditional waterfall.

There was one obstacle standing in their way though: Google. Google's ad server DoubleClick is responsible for delivering a lot of the ads you see on media owners' sites – and concerns were raised among media owners about a built-in bias which tended to give priority over buying impressions to Google's own ad exchange, AdX. That limited the buying pool, and therefore the CPMs that inventory could command. Eventually, media owners decided they'd had enough of Google's influence on their selling process… and so header bidding was born.

Header bidding is a sales method that basically disrupts the linear waterfall approach. It's called header bidding because it's done by placing a piece of code in the header tag of a page. Rather than each ad unit making a call to the ad server as it loads, the header tag loads first - identifying all the inventory on the page and making it available across multiple exchanges simultaneously. That means it'll go to the buyer who's willing to bid the most, regardless of whether they're in a PMP or on the open exchange, and independent of who that exchange is run by.

This is great in theory, but with so many different demand partners and exchanges out there that media owners might want to connect to, it can start getting pretty unwieldy pretty quickly. That's where header bidding wrappers come in. They work like a tag management system, allowing media owners to work with multiple demand-side partners easily. Plenty of companies, like Amazon A9, AppNexus and Index, now offer header bidding solutions that collate all the bids, so the page load isn't slowed significantly by calls being made to multiple exchanges and media owners don't have to worry about fostering relationships with unmanageable numbers of partners.

It didn't take Google long to realize that media owners were finding new routes to sale though – so they announced their exchange bidding dynamic allocation tool, or EBDA, which has essentially been billed as their alternative to header bidding, allowing the maximum bid price from each exchange – including Google's own – to compete fairly against one another so that the highest bid wins.

This shift on Google's part is reflective of a wider trend towards a fairer, more transparent and more premium way of trading programmatically. Trading within their own selection of PMPs lets media owners operate in a kind of halfway house between the security of direct deals and the buyer pool of the open exchange – and it gives the agencies and advertisers a level of control that they've been clamoring for, as we'll see later. As the programmatic market continues to develop, it looks like it will move more and more towards being cross-platform, clearer, more transparent and more direct – which is of benefit to everyone.

4.3.   Beyond display

As confidence in programmatic trading grows, media owners and advertisers alike have recognized that the opportunities it offers – convenient and automated connection of supply and demand, use of data and delivering meaningful, relevant creative – shouldn't be confined to the world of digital display. In fact, as long as it's bought, sold and delivered digitally, there's no reason why any form of media can't be traded programmatically.

Digital video formats have been traded programmatically for a while now. However, in recent years there's been something of a shift in what counts as 'digital video'. We're not just talking about inserting video content between two halves of an article any more -these days, TV content makes up a significant proportion of the digital video content watched by consumers. Whether that's catch-up services, on-demand platforms like Netflix, or even regular cable or satellite TV delivered via digital transmission methods -as long as digital's involved, there's the opportunity for TV formats to be traded programmatically.

While programmatic TV (or PTV) advertising is just another name for the technology- and data-driven trading of TV ad inventory, programmatic capabilities are allowing for newer, more advanced forms of TV ad targeting. Addressable TV is one example. Addressable TV ads are still bought against a particular audience segment - new mothers, for example -but instead of the same ads being shown to everyone in the ad breaks of shows often watched by that segment, real-time data is harnessed to deliver the ad impressions only to households who fit the targeting criteria, potentially showing a different ad to every household depending on the audience segment they belong to. At the moment this can only be done using special set-top boxes, but as technologies improve, we're likely to see more of this kind of TV advertising going forward.

Audio is another channel where programmatic trading has really taken off. With the growth of digital audio streaming platforms like Spotify and Apple Music there's been a massive increase in the amount of audio inventory available – plus these days 'traditional' radio stations have mostly transferred to digital delivery methods.

Spotify, for example, made their audio inventory available programmatically back in 2016, striking deals with SSPs AppNexus and Rubicon Project.

Plenty of programmatic audio exchanges have sprung up too – the Digital Audio Exchange is estimated to be the largest in Europe, and is integrated with major DSPs like

TubeMogul and AppNexus. In the US, Canada and Australia, Triton Digital's a2x audio exchange supports both open marketplace and private deals across more than 2000 live and on-demand audio stations.

Delivering audio programmatically has made dynamic audio ads a reality. In other words, you can record multiple component parts of an ad (different opening lines, or references to the listener's location, for example) and the final ad a listener actually hears will be made up of the components that are relevant for them.

Out of home technology has improved hugely in recent years, with advances in data collection thanks to beacons - which emit signals that can interact with your mobile device - and interactive facial recognition, which can be used to identify the age, gender and even facial expressions of people walking by to serve ads targeted to their profile. Combine this with all the other real-time data available – location, weather time of day and so on – and you can see why it's so attractive to be able to trade these formats programmatically. Out of home – like TV – has traditionally been a 'one to many' medium though, so any advertisers looking to use real-time data to make their creative relevant to consumers need to be aware of what consumers may or may not want displayed on a public billboard!

The final programmatic medium we're going to look at is print. This one's a bit different to the others we've talked about, because obviously print ads aren't delivered digitally! However, there are still opportunities to be gained from automating the buying and selling of print formats.

The difficulty in the automated trading of print inventory lies in the fact that, depending on the articles, the layout (or flatplan) of the publication shifts around with each edition – so there's never a guarantee of which ad formats will be available. The real-time element of programmatic should help with this, though – because in theory it allows publishers to offer their inventory as and when it becomes available.

Time Inc made headline news when they announced their decision to partner with MediaMath to make their audiences available to buy programmatically across both online and offline platforms. Unlike direct deals in print, the audience is bought across all Time Inc's properties on a CPM basis rather than through contact with individual titles. Ads on digital properties can be targeted to the same audience during the same period of a campaign as the print ads to maximize reinforcement of the message.

As you can see, programmatic trading is really making an impact across all kinds of media - and the market is likely to keep moving in this direction as more sellers and buyers recognize the appeal of trading programmatically.

5. Programmatic for agencies & publishers

Last time we saw how programmatic trading is actually done, and how far programmatic has come since the early days of buying and selling basic display ads. This time round, we'll look more at how programmatic has changed things for the companies and the people involve.

5.1. Programmatic for agencies

Programmatic, as we've seen, has had a pretty massive influence on virtually every area of the digital marketing landscape. The thing is, programmatic hasn't just changed trading methods – it's also fundamentally altered the structure of media agencies', media owners' and advertisers' businesses for the people who work there, and it's important to understand how.

We'll start with programmatic's impact on the agency world. The first big change programmatic brought to agency structures was the creation of the agency trading desk (or ATD).

ATDs were created by agency holding groups when they realized that programmatic buying was too big a task to be handled alongside anyone's pre-existing job.

Their job is to manage programmatic trading on behalf of all the agencies within the group – including managing agreements and relationships with multiple DSPs, using them to bid on inventory according to the parameters specified by the agency, maintaining and optimizing campaigns and reporting on campaign performance. ATDs may also buy large portions of premium inventory upfront, which they'll then repackage to sell on to their agency clients – effectively acting like a network.

For a time, ATDs tended to operate as separate entities from the main agencies - affiliated with, but distinguished from, their agency holding group. For example, Havas worked with Affiperf, Omnicom had Accuen and Publicis had Vivaki. It was actually Publicis and Vivaki that paved the way for this to change though, when they started to realize that areas like account management and analytics, which the ATDs were traditionally responsible for, had stopped existing independently and were now becoming much more integrated across the agency as a whole. It made sense for Vivaki's teams to follow suit; and so Vivaki became decentralized, with their programmatic experts now sitting as part of the digital teams across Publicis's agencies. Whereas not all ATDs have merged with their agencies – and they don't all perform identical functions – Publicis's move prompted more ATDs to integrate into the planning and buying teams of their respective agencies.

Agencies aren't the only group who've started to move programmatic expertise in-house. In fact, some advertisers and media owners are developing their own programmatic technology set-up - meaning that agencies are being pushed to offer additional services to retain their competitive edge. For many, this takes the form of consultative, advisory services – helping clients improve their technological expertise and leverage their own data better. In other words, the role of an agency is no longer just about planning and buying media.

As programmatic has revolutionized the agency world, the skillset required from an agency buyer has changed significantly too. They need to be a bit more tech-savvy than they might have been in the past (!) so that they can fully make the most of the technology that's now at their disposal – which includes being able to effectively analyze performance and interpret the results accordingly.

Although some brands are starting to take ownership of their own programmatic buying, it's unlikely that we'll ever see agencies being pushed out of the equation entirely. The vast majority of brands still turn to their agency partners for assistance in the buying process – because the agencies have established relationships with premium publishers in a way that advertisers, and the ad tech vendors they might turn to, just don't. Agencies can also negotiate better deals with publishers and DSPs because they're often buying large volumes of inventory at once. Basically, having programmatic capability doesn't just mean having access to the right technology; it also means having the human relationships required to leverage that technology in the best way.

5.2.   Programmatic for publishers

Agencies aren't the only ones who've been affected by the rise of programmatic. Media owners have been impacted too. Just like the agencies, publishers have needed to upskill significantly in the tech department if they want to sell their premium inventory for the best possible price on the programmatic market.

Some publishers – including Conde Nast, The Washington Post and The Guardian in the UK - have taken this one step further by choosing to develop their own Publisher Trading Desks. They were created in response to buyer demand for access to the media owner's audience in other places on the web. The PTDs buy inventory from elsewhere – other third-party sites or exchanges – and repackage it for resale, which is commonly referred to as audience extension. Sometimes they'll include their own inventory as part of these packages, but not always! This allows the publishers to offer a wider reach on a buyer's chosen audience – because they'll be able to target them in more places than just on the publisher's own site.

Of course, in doing this, publishers need to be wary of devaluing their own propositions. Yes, buyers are often after a high volume of inventory for a reasonable price – but by diluting your own premium inventory with low quality formats from dubious sources on the open exchange, you're probably doing more harm than good in the long run. If one of your clients believes they're getting guaranteed access to your premium audience and then sees their ad somewhere they didn't want it to show it up, you'll go down in their estimations pretty quickly! Most Publisher Trading Desks get around this by restricting their repackaged inventory to a pre-approved or 'whitelisted' selection of third parties — so they can be as transparent as possible when it comes to telling buyers what they'll be getting for their money.

Even if they're not operating a PTD, media owners will still need to choose the best programmatic sales channel for them, whether that's selling on the open exchange or running their own private marketplaces. We've seen that setting up PMPs can often be a good route to higher yields, but PMPs also require a significant amount of management. Media owners need to build and maintain relationships with the partners they want to

allow into their PMPs, they need to package inventory in a way that corresponds to their partners' needs — including offering cross-platform inventory bundles — and be able to accurately measure and report on these. In short, there are a lot of skills required to be able to run a PMP successfully.

Media owners have always needed to segment their audiences in order to be able to offer them up for sale. Programmatic trading has made this capability all the more significant — and media owners now need to be confident working with their own data to identify and accurately label their audiences. The more descriptive the labels, the better their chances of attracting the right buying partners — and it's more likely that these buyers will be willing to pay higher prices if they can clearly see that the audience segment meets their criteria.

All of this means that the day-to-day activity of a media owner has changed somewhat since the advent of programmatic, and so have the skills needed for the job. Programmatic specialists, data scientists and analysts are all crucial parts of a media owner's team nowadays. You'll notice that media owners don't generally divide their sales teams according to programmatic or non-programmatic functions. Instead, what's needed is a level of expertise across the board, so that advertisers and agencies all go through one sales team regardless of how they're buying.

In fact, the relationship between media owners and the buy-side is a crucial component in programmatic trading – and despite the introduction of technologies to help automate the process, a lot of this relationship is still conducted face-to-face. Many of the higher yielding programmatic strategies require back-and-forth communication – so media owner sales teams need to be prepared to discuss their programmatic offering in person with everyone they speak to, from communications planners to experienced programmatic traders.

5.3.   Programmatic for advertisers

From an advertiser's point of view, the early days of programmatic were a difficult time. Early programmatic trading methods are sometimes referred to as 'black box', because it was very difficult to see exactly what was going on inside 'the programmatic machine' – advertisers would find themselves unsure of where their money was going, where their ads had ended up, and whether they were actually having an impact!

As a result, transparency quickly became a key theme in the market, and we'll hear more about that later on. One way that advertisers tried to gain more control over what was actually happening to their ads was to bring programmatic solutions in-house. This basically translates to advertisers doing their own programmatic buying, rather than employing an external agency to help. So instead, the advertiser is responsible for establishing their own relationships with DSPs, setting up and maintaining their own campaigns and developing their own buying strategies.

It's worth saying at this point that bringing programmatic in-house is a pretty big undertaking, so it tends to only be the really big advertisers who decide to take it on - and even they will usually have backing from large consultancy groups like Accenture to help them set up and manage their own in-house trading desks.

Unilever and P&G are two global advertisers who've made the move to bring programmatic buying in-house. They have the scale to justify spending on programmatic technology, as well as the first party data to define their target audiences accurately. As part of their strategy, Unilever also handle relationships with multiple DSPs depending on the kind of data they're using. If it's their own first party data, they'll segment it using their own licensed DMP and then they'll control which DSP and ad server they use. They still have a media agency on board when they work with third party data though.

P&G's in-house programmatic strategy is slightly different. They partner with third party tech vendors like Neustar and The Trade Desk to run their Hawkeye trading platform, which gives P&G greater visibility into their own transactions, as well as keeping their buying separate from other brands who share their agency - and therefore their ATD.

Unless you've got the resource to handle it though, bringing programmatic in-house isn't really going to solve any advertisers' concerns about transparency or visibility. That's why most advertisers will find themselves deciding between a managed solution or a media agency for access to a DSP. Managed solutions are where, instead of relying on the media agency to foster a relationship with a DSP, the advertiser chooses a DSP that includes an account management team within their programmatic offering, who'll handle the set-up and day-to-day activity for you. If you do decide to go down that route, it'll require close collaboration with your account team over at the DSP to define strategies, objectives, target audiences, and media owners you want to work with.

With all these different options, and so many DSPs out there, how do advertisers actually choose which tech vendors to work with? It might be that the DSP plugs into a lot of different exchanges, meaning they have access to a wide range of inventory.

Or maybe they've got particular expertise in a certain part of the market. There are practical concerns too - price and budget will always be a factor.

The main thing advertisers need to be aware of if their programmatic buying isn't being done in-house is that they can't just hand over the specifications to their media agency or ad tech partner and then wash their hands of it. Any good programmatic partner will be reporting regularly on the performance of your ads, including how well they're doing with different audiences – and you need to be ready to adapt your strategy based on what these reports say. There's often an element of 'test and learn' in this process as you work to optimize your ads for the right audience, testing frequency levels, different creatives and so on.

One thing that can make this process slightly smoother is for advertisers to collect their own first party data. Collecting data straight from the user – when they subscribe to a newsletter, or register to buy products, for example – can help the advertiser to create much more sophisticated, detailed target audience definitions to be entered into their DSP.

Say you're a high-end jewelry brand, so you want your ads to reach an audience of high-earners. Your DSP will probably connect you to media owners like The Wall Street Journal where this audience can typically be found. However, if you've collected first party data, you can refine the Wall Street Journal's 'high earners' audience segment to only target people who've shopped with you before, or who've signed up to receive information from you.

First party data can also be used to identify 'lookalike audiences', who share qualities with the people who've given you their data before. Whether they share interests, behaviors or demographics, targeting people who are similar to your previous customers is a great way of addressing people who are likely to become customers in future.

What we're seeing, then, is that programmatic isn't about flicking a switch and allowing the technology to do all the work for you. Advertisers need to be constantly aware of the changes in the market and willing to respond to them – whether that's changing tech providers, upskilling staff or altering focus. Entering into the programmatic space is a long- term commitment – but the reason we're seeing it become commonplace is that its benefits make all this effort worthwhile.

6. Themes in programmatic

Programmatic, as we've seen, is a fast-moving landscape where new risks, issues – and ultimately, solutions! – are being identified all the time. When programmatic trends change, it often makes a big splash in the industry - and it's important to keep up with what's going on, as changes can often have a major effect on your programmatic activity, whichever side of the sales partnership you sit on!

We've spent most of these sections talking about programmatic inventory, but the growth of programmatic has meant that ad spots and formats aren't the only things being traded any more. There's a growing demand from agencies to be able to access decoupled data from media owners. In other words, they want to buy the data that media owners have on their audiences, without having to buy the inventory that would normally come along with it.

There are two main reasons an agency might want to buy decoupled data. Firstly, if they're buying and repackaging inventory through an agency trading desk, they can combine the decoupled data with the data they already have – making it easier to find the same audience across multiple sites and therefore using it to inform their buying strategy. Or they might just be looking to purchase media owner data to use across their media plan, outside of the media owner's platform, which adds value to the agency's proposition, especially if this is signed in first party data, which has traditionally been something that clients can only get from the media owner themselves.

Of course, media owners are well aware of the value that their audience data carries, and so not all of them have been keen to share it without selling it in the context of their inventory. It's understandable that they've approached it with caution – after all, it gives agencies and advertisers a way to target the media owner's audience, without having to actually purchase the media owner's inventory or serve ads on the media owner's site to do so!

Some media owners have made the move towards data decoupling though, and it can provide a useful revenue stream for those concerned about ad blocking. UK publisher The Guardian, for example, offers data on either off-the-shelf or bespoke audience segments to trusted partners. Of course, privacy laws surrounding data are a big concern, so if you're a media owner who's looking to start selling decoupled data, make sure you've done your homework first!

Another major concern for those who've seen programmatic's influence grow over the years is: just how much of what advertisers, media owners and media agencies do will eventually be automated? As we've already seen, face-to-face human relationships are still a crucial part of the programmatic process, and that's definitely not going to change any time soon. What we are likely to see is an increase in the use of machine learning to help with the automation of programmatic campaigns – but this will be in the more laborious, mundane areas of programmatic, like gathering data on campaign performance and producing reports. There'll still be a need for people to be involved, because while a machine can gather data on how many clicks your ads are receiving

from different audiences and present this in a nice graph, it can't tell you why you might be under- or overperforming or what you should do to fix it. That's something that only a human will ever be able to do; so, although job specs and the skills needed might change as automation improves, programmatic technology is definitely not going to be taking humans out of the equation!

We've touched on the issues around brand safety and transparency already. Especially for buyers in the open marketplace, there's a real concern among advertisers that programmatic buying can lead to their brand being displayed in the wrong places. If you think about the number of impressions being sold on a daily basis, and all the different marketplaces and exchanges they might pass through on their way to being sold, it's no wonder that – even with precautions in place – it's difficult to monitor whether they're meeting the brand's exact requirements. Brand safety isn't just a concern for advertisers either; media owners have a reputation to protect too, and allowing poor quality, annoying or inappropriate ads to appear alongside their content can be severely damaging.

There are many environments that might be unsafe for a brand to appear in. They could be contextually irrelevant – an ad for a new chocolate bar appearing on a healthy eating website, for example. Or it could be a lot worse. Some brands have found their ads appearing on websites containing extremist content. Not only is this incredibly damaging to your brand's reputation – it also means that the money you're spending on your ads is funding the creators of these websites.

So, what can you do? Most media owners and advertisers will operate some kind of 'blacklist', which prevents certain parties from trading with them. The problem is that building a blacklist requires someone to manually process all the sites that could match your targeting criteria – and with the sheer volume of new sites that spring up every single day, it's unrealistic to expect you'll ever manage to list them all. Instead, many advertisers have opted for a 'whitelisting' approach where they'll select a network of sites

that they do want to buy inventory from, and automatically exclude the rest. This approach can reduce the threat to brand safety – but the real key is to get transparency from your programmatic trading partners.

Since advertisers became aware of the brand safety issues associated with programmatic, there's been an increased demand for transparency in the market. P&G have really been at the forefront of this, pushing their agencies to only work with vendors that have been accredited by the Media Rating Council and with media owners who agree to third party verification. These days, very few advertisers would accept a contract with limited transparency in return for a guaranteed outcome. Now it's far more important to know where your ads are ending up and be sure that the people who are viewing or clicking on them are the audience you're actually after.

The other issue related to transparency is cost. As an impression moves through the programmatic ecosystem, it's passed across multiple platforms – SSPs, DSPs, ad servers, and so on. Unsurprisingly, the providers of each of these platforms require a fee – usually either a percentage of the CPM or a fixed price per impression, although advertisers traditionally haven't been given a very clear overview of how these prices are calculated. All these individual fees can add up quite quickly, and they're sometimes referred to as a 'tech tax'. Just as advertisers now look for transparency when it comes to where their ads are appearing, they also want to know where their ads are going along the way – and, more importantly, how much of their budget is actually going on inventory as opposed to paying various tech vendors' fees.

Of course, if you've got your own tech then you avoid paying at least some of these fees – but, as we've discussed, that's not a viable solution for the vast majority of advertisers. Some ad tech companies like AOL have worked on developing their own tech ecosystem to save advertisers having to pay fees to multiple companies; but that risks becoming too dependent on a single trading platform, which is something that both buyers and sellers usually try to avoid.

To try to solve this problem, a number of advertisers have opted for a hybrid model, where they build their own in-house programmatic ecosystem without trying to take on everything - so they might have their own trading desk and direct relationships with an ad server, but still partner with a media agency when it comes to decisions on planning or strategy.

The final issue we're going to tackle is data leakage. Any media owner who wants to trade their inventory programmatically will need to install tags on their page that can collect and communicate data back to the relevant parties – placing a call to an ad server, segmenting the user and so on.

Generally speaking, these tags will belong to the third parties they're communicating with – meaning that the site's owner doesn't know how they were built or what they were built to do. That means that, as well as the data they need to collect to make the programmatic process run smoothly, these tags may also be gathering extra data on behalf of the third party without the publisher's knowledge.

It's rare that this kind of data leakage happens due to malicious intent from the third party, though it can happen! Most companies who collect publisher data through their tags are open about it – it's just that media owners don't always have a clear process in place for integrating third party vendors' products into their site, or for assuring that the third party's terms align with their wider business strategy. If lots of individual departments have integrated various third-party tags, it can be easy to lose central oversight of what's being used and for what purposes. The real concern with this is that, if media owners are giving their data away for free, they lose a lot of what gives their proposition real value.

However, don't forget that anyone selling leaked media owner data will have to sell it as third-party data. There's a lot of third-party data available in the market from plenty of different sources, so these companies can't really use leaked data as a way to differentiate themselves from the crowd. Plus, as soon as first party data becomes third party data, it loses a lot of its value, because getting first party data straight from the media owner who collected it gives you a certain guarantee that it'll be both unique and accurate - so agencies and advertisers generally prefer to obtain first party data.

That means that media owners who are worried about data leakage should look to offer their data for sale themselves, at a price they feel reflects its true value. Those who do are more than likely to get buyers coming directly to them rather than getting hold of it through third party sources. Even if media owners aren't comfortable with selling their data, they can still sell insights or research that reflects what that data shows.

There's always a lot going on in the programmatic space, and it can sometimes seem that with every challenge overcome, a new one appears in its place! The main thing to realize is that the market is progressing towards a fairer, safer and more transparent way of trading programmatically, allowing advertisers, media agencies and media owners alike to really benefit from all the opportunities it has to offer.

7. Glossary

Ad Exchange is an automated system which facilitates the buying and selling of advertising space, often (but not always) through real-time bidding (RTB).

Ad Impression is a single ad that appears on a web page. Because several ads often appear on the same web page, the number of registered ad impressions will almost always exceed the number of page impressions.

Ad Network is a platform that aggregates the inventory of lots of different media owners to sell to the buyside, with pricing based on each website's audience profile.

Ad Verification is a service which enables advertisers to confirm that their ads have been delivered into the intended content.

Attribution Modelling is a plan for distributing credit for a user's conversion amongst the various channels or touchpoints they have come in contact with prior to purchase.

Cost per Action (CPA) is a pricing model where the advertiser pays the online advertiser if an action, such as a sale or a registration, results from a user's exposure to the advertising. It is mostly used by direct response advertisers.

Cost per Click (CPC) is the amount an advertiser pays the online publisher each time a user clicks on their ad. The CPC is affected by several factors, including how much competition there is in the market.

Cost per Impression (CPI) means that advertisers pay for the number of times their ad is displayed.

Data Management Platform (DMP) is a piece of software that warehouses and analyses audience data for media companies. DMPs are often used to manage Deal IDs and create audience segments for targeting purposes.

Data Providers collect and sell information that can help advertisers decide on the placement of their ads and what ads they'll use.

Demand Side Platforms (DSPs) are technologies which enable buyers to manage their bids for ad inventory bought via exchanges. In addition, the tracking, optimization and ad serving capabilities of these platforms enable buyers to make huge efficiencies in terms of cost and return on investment.

Display Ads is a type of multimedia advertising which often uses images (static and moving), sound and text. Banner ads, MPUs/Medium Rectangles and Skyscrapers are typical display ad formats, although formats are continuously evolving. Display ads are very different from classified or search ads, which are typically text-based.

Programmatic Trading is the automated buying and selling of ads in real-time.

Ghost site are real websites with actual content; however, the content is often low-quality or stolen. These sites only exist to create more ad inventory that can be sold, and often, botnets are responsible for the traffic or impressions reported.

Pixel Stuffing is a type of ad fraud in which a spot is placed in a 1x1 pixel so that, when an ad is served, an impression is reported, but the ad is too small to actually be seen on the page

Publisher runs the sites and advertises the product or service to users, driving them to making a purchase.

Supply Side Platforms (SSPs) Technologies are technologies which enable sellers to locate the highest prices for their ad inventory within multiple ad exchanges.

Viewability is the measurement of how much of an ad appears on a user's screen, and for how long. This measurement is then used to determine whether an ad has had the opportunity to be seen by the user it was served to.

Viewable Cost Per Mille (vCPM) is a payment model in which advertisers pay a set price for one thousand impressions that meet standards for viewability. This is in contrast to cost per mille, or CPM, in which an advertiser pays a set price for one thousand impressions, regardless of whether or not those impressions were viewable.

8. Other books of the series

Delphiki, J. (2020). *eCommerce 360: Start your Online Business, Create your eCommerce and Sell on Marketplaces.*

Delphiki, J. (2020). *Social Media Business: Define your social media strategy, start selling on social media and expand your business in China.*

Delphiki, J. (2020). *Web Analytics & Big Data: Improve your e-Commerce metrics, online insights to sell.*

Printed in Great Britain
by Amazon

50128981R00047